THE BEST ME! HEALTH

Max Your Health!

by
Kimmie Auntie

Illustrations by
Ayeshe Sadr & Ishaan Dasgupta

another title brought to you from
the **BEST ME** series

SCHOLASTIC
New York Toronto London Auckland
Sydney New Delhi Hong Kong

For my real-life Max, in gratitude for our wild rumpus life that he makes so abundant.

Published by Scholastic India Pvt. Ltd.
A subsidiary of Scholastic Inc., New York, 10012 (USA).
Publishers since 1920, with international operations in Canada, Australia, New Zealand, the United Kingdom, India, and Hong Kong.

For information regarding permission, write to:
Scholastic India Pvt. Ltd.
A-27, Ground Floor, Sigma Centre
Infocity-1, Sector 34, Gurgaon 122001 (India)

This edition: October 2022

ISBN-13: 978-93-8610-676-6

Printed in India Sterling Graphics Pvt. Ltd., Manesar

Dear friend,
Here's the thing—whether you are healthy or not is your choice. Mom and Dad can urge you to live well (and maybe even force you for a few more years) but finally, it is up to you. Yup, you!

If you want to live the richness life has to offer—if you want to think sharp and play hard and love well—being healthy makes it all better. Eat those vegetables. Exercise. Sleep enough. Enjoy toffees—just not too many!

Max your HEALTH!

Truly,
Kimmie Auntie

TATA DA
DAAAAA!

"Good books!"
he yelled with a twirl.
"Kind thoughts!"
he hollered with his
cape fluttering.
"A soft heart!"
he sang as he shimmied about.

(Superheroes are very active.)

"But, Mom, you know the best part of keeping things *IN*?"

"What's that, Max?"

"YOU! Keeping family *IN* is very healthy."

And Max gave
his Mom a big
SUPERHERO
hug.

Discussion Questions for Parents and Teachers:

What does it mean to be healthy?

Why do we ____? (brush our teeth, take a bath, drink water, exercise)

Why does a parent or adult care if their child is healthy? (i.e. a parent is not mean to set limits around how much toffee or TV a child can have—they love them and want what's best!)

Tell me a time that you chose to be healthy? (or ask specifically ... protected your body from germs, etc.)

Why is setting good patterns of healthy behaviour now important for your whole life?

Activities:

1. Take a paper plate and let the children draw healthy things to eat on the plate. Use this as a discussion starter.

2. Draw a chalk circle on the ground and label *IN* or *OUT*. Have the child hop back and forth as you call out things that are healthy or not.

3. Have your child draw a SUPERHERO GATE logo and post it on your gate, bedroom door or somewhere they get reminded.

4. Have the child sing a song as they wash their hands (to ensure the recommended 20 seconds it requires to be clean).

5. Make a SUPERHERO GATE cape and watch your little superhero bounce about!

*Parenting Tip: Ask your child "What are some things we should keep *IN* and what are some things we should keep OUT?" Help your child make a list in addition to the ones in the story. When you want to encourage a child to choose wisely, ask them, "Should this be *IN* or OUT?" or "Where's the SUPERHERO GATE?"